THE PUMPKIN BOOK

Full of Halloween
History, Poems, Songs
Art Projects, Games and Recipes

For Parents and Teachers
to use with
young Children

Written and Illustrated
by
Susan Olson Higgins

Ask for these additional Holiday Books
by the same Author:
THE THANKSGIVING BOOK
THE BUNNY BOOK
THE ELVES' CHRISTMAS BOOK

PUMPKIN PRESS

P.O. Box 139
Shasta, CA 96087

6th Edition, Copyright © 1983, Susan Olson Higgins
Revised Edition © 1984, by Susan Olson Higgins

Written and Published by Susan Olson Higgins
P.O. Box 139, Shasta, CA 96087

*Dedicated to all the
Happy Halloweens
on Randall Avenue ...
and to
Danny
Peter
and
Joshua
with all my love.*

An enormous heartfelt thank you to Linda Jones, Jane Williams, Susan Lynch, Ruth Mudder, and especially Susan Pittleman and V.I. Wexner for editing and watering the pumpkin.

PREFACE

Halloween is one of the most exciting holidays of the year. Children love it and so do I. So I have written and gathered Halloween history, lore, poems, songs, art projects, games, and recipes for you to use this season to have the most pumpkinny Halloween ever! Enjoy!

Susan Olson Higgins

TABLE OF CONTENTS

A Pumpkin History of Halloween 4
Pumpkin Trivia 6
Pumpkin Roots 7
Pumpkin Poems 8

    Goblins 9
    Who's Afraid? 10
    October 10
    Little Ghost 11
    It's Halloween Night 12
    The Skeleton Is Up 13
    The Goblin 13
    What Is It? 14
    Five Little Pumpkins 14
    Jack-O'-Lantern 15
    Riddle: What Am I? 15
    Funny Pumpkin 15
    Can You Guess? 16
    Who Am I? 16
    Tonight Is Halloween 17
    Halloween Mask 17
    Five Little Goblins 18
    Halloween Action Poem .18
    Old Witch 19
    A Big Black Bat 20
    Isn't Halloween Fun? 20
    Halloween Song 21

PUMPKIN SONGS TO TUNES YOU KNOW ...22

Fat Little Pumpkin 23
Tonight Is Halloween 25
Halloween Is Here...............................26
Here Comes Halloween...........................27
The Ghost Is Here To Play.......................28
I'm A Jack-O'-Lantern 29
Did You Ever See A Goblin?.....................30

PUMPKIN ART 31

Pumpkin Totem Pole 32
Tear A Ghost....................................33
Plant Your Pumpkin Seeds 33
Finger Paint A Pumpkin 34
A Cat Behind A Pumpkin........................34
Mask On A Stick 35
Weave A Halloween Placemat 35
Halloween Owl 36
Halloween Tree 36
Pumpkin In A Window 37
Mouse Puzzle In A Pumpkin 38
Cotton Ghosts In A Haunted House 39
Charcoal A Goblin 40
Bean Bag Ghost.................................40
Black Cat Noise Makers 41
Play Dough Pumpkin Patch 42
Sew A Ghost....................................43
Pumpkin Finger Puppets 44
Stuff A Witch 45

PUMPKIN GAMES 46

    Witch, Where's Your Broom? 47

    Spin The Halloween Bottle 48

    Halloween Match 49

    Put The Felt Nose On The Pumpkin 50

    Halloween Sequence Posters 50

    Hide The Ghost 51

    Pass The Pumpkins 51

    Tell A Pumpkin Tale 52

    Witches, Ghosts and Goblins 53

PUMPKIN TREATS 54

    Aunt Linda's Sugar Cookie Ghosts 55

    Fried Pumpkin Seeds 56

    Cream Cheese Ghosts with Crackers 57

    Peanut Ghosts 58

    Halloween Punch 58

    Pumpkin Soup 59

    Pumpkin Bread 60

    Caramel Apples 61

    Pumpkin Pancakes 62

    Susan's Tootsie Roll Ghosts 63

WHAT IS REAL? WHAT IS PRETEND? 64

YOUR OWN PUMPKIN NOTES 65

THE PUMPKIN HISTORY OF HALLOWEEN

In medieval times, October 31 was a holy night known as All Hallows Eve. It was the evening before All Saints' Day. In ancient Britain and Ireland, the Celtic festival of Samhain was observed on October 31. That date also marked the eve of the new year during Celtic and Anglo-Saxon times. The new year was welcomed with huge bonfires set on hilltops to frighten away evil spirits. October 31 was also a time for returning herds from the pasture, and renewing laws and land-leases.

Traditionally, it was believed that ghosts, hobgoblins, witches, fairies, black cats, and demons were roaming about on this day, and it was the time that the souls of the dead were to revisit their homes. It was also a time to make peace with the supernatural powers controlling nature. It was a favorable time to predict futures and interpret omens concerning marriages, luck, health, and death. It was the only day on which the help of the devil was requested. No wonder we associate witches, ghosts, goblins and other supernatural spirits with Halloween today.

Gradually, over the years, Halloween became a secular observance. Many different customs and practices developed. For example, in Scotland young people came together to play games to determine which of them would marry during the coming year and in what order the marriages would occur. I am sure those parties were full of laughter and fun.

Halloween became popular in the United States during the late 19th Century. Young men and boys would pull mischievous pranks and sometimes cause extensive damage. Later, Halloween was observed primarily by the young children who went from door to door in costume asking for a trick or a treat. Candy was usually given to the children; and still is today.

PUMPKIN TRIVIA

Today, a common symbol of Halloween is the jack-o'-lantern. This is a hollowed-out pumpkin carved in the appearance of a demon's face or a jolly clown with a candle lighted inside. At one time it was set out to scare off evil spirits, although today it is used merely for decoration. Originally, in Scotland a turnip was used. But since the turnips in the United States were too small to hold a candle, a native pumpkin was substituted.

The jack-o'-lantern was probably named after the night watchman who, long ago, carried a candle inside a lantern to shed light as he walked the streets of a town making sure that all was quiet and all was well. The candle inside a pumpkin resembled the night watchman's lantern. (So that was how, most likely, the jack-o'-lantern earned its name.)

PUMPKIN ROOTS

How can you grow a pumpkin? Well, in the spring, find a sunny spot in the garden. Plant a few pumpkin seeds in a little mound of soil. Water them regularly. Soon, tangled vines with broad prickly leaves will sprout and grow over the mound. Two or three yellow flowers will blossom on each vine. Then tiny pumpkins will begin to form in place of the blossoms. The pumpkins will slowly grow bigger and plumper every day. In the fall, they will be ready to harvest. We can thank the Indians for our ample, orange colored pumpkins. Long ago they conscientiously cultivated the large pumpkins we enjoy today.

Most pumpkins weigh between 9 and 18 pounds, although some varieties can grow to weigh up to 100 pounds. Pumpkins are usually picked by hand, then used to make pumpkin pie, pumpkin soup, pumpkin pudding, a vegetable for the table, or feed for the livestock. But if a pumpkin is lucky, it will be meticulously choosen, hollowed out, carved, and proudly displayed on Halloween with a candle lit inside. It will become a jolly jack-o'-lantern.

Pumpkin Poems

GOBLINS by Susan Olson Higgins

Red goblins, yellow goblins,
Blue and green,
These are the funniest
I have ever seen.

Tramping out along the street
Knocking at each door,
It looks to me like Halloween
Has come once more!

WHO'S AFRAID? by Susan Olson Higgins

I'm a little ghost who's all about.
I fly in and I fly out.
Don't be afraid of what I do
'Cause on Halloween, I'm afraid of you!

OCTOBER by Elsie Towler

Did you ever see an old witch riding through the sky?
You did? So did I!
Did you ever feel a white thing gliding through the air?
You did? What a scare!
Did you ever see a cat's eye, shining in the night?
You did? What a fright!
Did you ever hear a night owl crying, "Whoo-oo-oo"?
You did? I did too!
Did you think that I was scared at what I'd seen?
Not a bit. It's Halloween!

LITTLE GHOST by Susan Olson Higgins

Sh-h-h-h-h-h-h
Little ghost, little ghost,
You're so quiet as you go,
Little ghost, little ghost,
Invisible head to toe.

Little ghost, little ghost,
I'm not afraid of you,
Little ghost, little ghost,
Not of anything you do.

Little ghost, little ghost,
You fly so fast and far,
Little ghost, little ghost,
Will you catch me a star?

Little ghost, little ghost,
So you can hold the light,
Little ghost, little ghost,
On every Halloween night.

Little ghost, little ghost,
Then I'll know where you are,
Little ghost, little ghost,
When I see that twinkling star.

11

IT'S HALLOWEEN NIGHT

by Susan Olson Higgins

Put on your costume,
Tie your mask on tight.
Grab your bag for trick-or-treating
'Cause it's Halloween night!

THE SKELETON IS UP!

by Susan Olson Higgins

Knock, knock, knicker, knocker, clink, clank, clunk.
I hear that skeleton in the attic trunk.

Click, click, clunk, clunk, clicker, clacker, clup,
That old skeleton is finally getting up.

Knick, knick, knack, knack, knock, knock, knocker,
I will sit and wait for him in my squeaky rocker.

Clunk, clunk, click, clack, knick, knack, knor,
That klacky skeleton is clunking out the door.

Knicker, knocker, knack, knack, knick, knock, kneen,
The skeleton is out! It's time for Halloween!

THE GOBLIN from the French

A goblin lives in our house,
In our house, in our house.
A goblin lives in our house,
All the year round.

He bumps, he jumps,
And he stumps,
He knocks and he rocks,
And he rattles at the locks.

A goblin lives in our house,
In our house, in our house,
A goblin lives in our house
All the year round.

13

WHAT IS IT? by Aileen Fisher

It isn't two — it's only one,
and yet, we use it twice.

It's round and fat and full of fun
because it's doubly nice.

In fall it has an honored place,
and I will tell you why:

Its outside makes a smiling face,
Its inside makes a pie!

What is it?

FIVE LITTLE PUMPKINS
by Unknown Author

Five little pumpkins sitting on a gate.
The first one said, "Oh my, it's getting late."
The second one said, "there are witches in the air."
The third one said, "But we don't care."
The fourth one said, "Let's run, let's run."
The fifth one said, "It's Halloween fun."
Then "Woo-oo-oo" went the wind,
And out went the lights,
Those five little pumpkins,
Ran out of sight.

14

JACK-O'-LANTERN

by Susan Olson Higgins

I was a pumpkin big and round
When I grew upon the ground.
Now I have a mouth and nose
And two eyes that never close.
Light my candle on Halloween
So that my jolly face is seen
By every ghost and witch and cat
And trick-or-treating acrobat.
I will smile and shine for you
If you come trick-or-treating, too!

RIDDLE: WHAT AM I?

by Dorothy Aldis

They chose me from my brothers:
"That's the nicest one," they said,
And they carved me out a face
And put a candle in my head;

And they set me on the doorstep.
Oh, the night was dark and wild;
But when they lit the candle,
Then I smiled!

FUNNY PUMPKIN by Unknown Author

I made a funny pumpkin
For everyone to see.
It looked so big and terrible
It even frightened me!

CAN YOU GUESS?

by Susan Olson Higgins

Way out back where the pumpkins grow,
Sitting on the shoulder of the old scarecrow,
A feathery friend caws high and low,
He's a black and noisy Halloween...*(crow)*.

Floating quietly through the air
You're not sure if he's here or there,
You can't see him, but he's friendly to most,
You can guess! He's a Halloween...*(ghost)*

You might hear a cackle or a broom sweep by
As she flies toward the moon riding high in the sky.
She'll sail right over a mountain or a ditch.
She is known as a Halloween...*(witch)*

WHO AM I?

by Unknown Author

A face so round
And eyes so bright
A nose that glows
My, what a sight.
A scary mouth
With a jolly grin
No arms, no legs,
Just head to chin.

16

TONIGHT IS HALLOWEEN

by Susan Olson Higgins

You step out into darkness
And you look all around.
Something is going to get you,
You know it by the sound.
And then you feel a shiver
Slide up and down your spine,
You look in all the bushes
But there's not a single sign.

Then all of a sudden,
From out behind a tree,
One little Pirate jumps
And yells, "It's only me!
Come on! Let's go trick-or-treating!
Pretend we're scary and mean.
This is ghost and goblin night.
Tonight is Halloween!!"

HALLOWEEN MASK

by Susan Olson Higgins

Pull it over your face,
Just your eyes peek through.
Now you can smile and giggle
When your friends say, "Who are you?"

FIVE LITTLE GOBLINS

by Susan Olson Higgins

Five little goblins, funny little men,
Chase under moonlight in the globlins' glen.

One little goblin knocked on witch's door,
The witch opened up, now there are four.

Four little goblins underneath a tree,
One climbed the branches, now there only
three.

Three little goblins wondering what to do,
One went to see the Elves, now there are two.

Two little goblins, Halloween fun,
One hopped in the pumpkin patch, now there is
one.

One little goblin said, "Watch me run
Over to the scarecrow," now there are none.

HALLOWEEN ACTION POEM

by Susan Olson Higgins

Flap your wings like a big black bat,
Arch your back like a witch's cat.
Prowl around like a goblin on the town,
Dance on tiptoes like a funny, floppy clown.
Fly away on your magic broomstick,
Open your bag for a treat or a trick.
Float through the air like a ghost all about,
Now everyone together, let me hear you shout,
                    HAPPY HALLOWEEN!

OLD WITCH by Unknown Author

There's a strange old witch
In a pointed hat
Who rides on a broom
With her big black cat
Across the sky
When the moon is fat
On the night of Halloween

A BIG BLACK BAT by Susan Olson Higgins

A big black bat comes flying through the night.
As he zoomed right past me, it was quite a scary sight!
But I don't care if he's prowling in the air,
I'm safe and sound...hiding underneath the chair.

ISN'T HALLOWEEN FUN?

by Susan Olson Higgins

Wee little brownies and flying black bats,
Witches on broomsticks with tall pointed hats,
Gay jack-o'-lanterns sitting all about,
Laughing and whispering, "The children are out!"

Doorbells are ringing, the moon is getting high,
Goblins and elves are tiptoeing by
Spooks at the windows peek and then they run.
Oh me, oh my! Isn't Halloween fun?

HALLOWEEN SONG by Marjorie Barrows

Three little witches
Pranced in the garden,
Three little witches
Danced from the moon.
One wore a wishing hat,
One held a pussy-cat,
One went a-pitty-pat
And whispered a tune.

Out flew an owl
Who glared at the kitten,
Out flew an owl
Who stared at the rest,
Dancing, with haughty nose
Each on the other's toes,
Down past the pumpkin rows
Under his nest.

Three little witches
Blew on their broomsticks,
Three little witches
Flew to their queen,
Over the windy glen
Into the night...But then
They will be back again
Next Halloween.

Pumpkin Songs

To Tunes You Know

THE FAT LITTLE PUMPKIN

by Susan Olson Higgins
(tune: Way Down Yonder In The Paw Paw Patch)

I was a fat little pumpkin,
I was a fat little pumpkin,
I was a fat little pumpkin,
Way down yonder in the pumpkin patch.

One little girl (or: one little boy)
Came and picked me,
One little girl came and picked me,
One little girl came and picked me,
Way down yonder in the pumpkin patch.

Now I'm Jolly Jack-O'-Lantern,
Now I'm Jolly Jack-O'-Lantern,
Now I'm Jolly Jack-O'-Lantern,
Smiling at my friends in the pumpkin patch.

24

TONIGHT IS HALLOWEEN

by Susan Olson Higgins
(tune: Mulberry Bush)

Dance around the witch's hat,
Dance around the witch's hat,
Dance around the witch's hat,
Tonight is Halloween

Tiptoe 'round the goblin's shoe,
Tiptoe 'round the goblin's shoe,
Tiptoe 'round the goblin's shoe,
Tonight is Halloween.

Hop over the black cat's tail,
Hop over the black cat's tail,
Hop over the black cat's tail,
Tonight is Halloween.

Whish-whoosh a ghost was here,
Whish-whoosh a ghost was here,
Whish-whoosh a ghost was here,
Tonight is Halloween.

Clap to chase them all away,
Clap to chase them all away,
Clap to chase them all away,
Tonight is Halloween.

Now it's time to trick-or-treat,
Now it's time to trick-or-treat,
Now it's time to trick-or-treat,
Tonight is Halloween.

HALLOWEEN IS HERE

by Susan Olson Higgins
(tune: Down By The Station)

Down by the old tree underneath a full moon,
There the witches gather with their magic brooms.
The old owl hooted, the bats begin to flutter,
    Who-o-o, Who-o-o, Flap, Flap
Halloween is here.

Down by the river in between the cattails,
Ghosts are floating gently on the misty air.
A soft breeze is blowing, stars begin to twinkle,
    F-f-f-f, F-f-f-f, Blink, Blink,
Halloween is here.

Down by the red barn in between the cornstalks,
Sits a little pumpkin fat as he can be.
A little mouse comes creeping in beside the pumpkin,
    Whisper, Whisper,
Halloween is here.

Back in the white house you can hear the chatter,
Kids are getting ready for a special night.
They're putting on their costumes, then visiting the neighbors,
    Knock, Knock, Trick-or-Treat,
Halloween is here!

HERE COMES HALLOWEEN

by Susan Olson Higgins
(tune: Ten Little Indians)

Here come all the pumpkins,
Here come all the pumpkins,
Here come all the pumpkins,
With their yellow light.

Here come all the witches,
Here come all the witches,
Here come all the witches,
Flying through the night.

Here come all the goblins,
Here come all the goblins,
Here come all the goblins,
With smiles so big and bright.

Here come all the children,
Here come all the children,
Here come all the children,
Such a happy sight.

THE GHOST IS HERE TO PLAY

by Susan Olson Higgins
(tune: Farmer In The Dell)

The ghost is here to play,
The ghost is here to play,
Hi, Ho! It's Halloween,
The ghost is here to play.

The ghost picks a witch,
The ghost picks a witch,
Hi, Ho! It's Halloween,
The ghost picks a witch.

Additional verses...

> The witch picks a bat...
> The bat picks a skeleton...
> The skeleton picks a cat...
> The cat picks a child...
> The child picks a pumpkin...
> The pumpkin stands alone...

I'M A JACK-O'-LANTERN

by Susan Olson Higgins
(tune: I'm A Little Teapot)

I'm a jack-o'-lantern,
Fat and fine.
They picked me off a pumpkin vine.

Halloween is coming,
Don't you know.
Just light my candle and watch me glow.

DID YOU EVER SEE A GOBLIN?

by Susan Olson Higgins
(tune: Did You Ever See A Lassie?)

Did you ever see a goblin,
A goblin, a goblin?
Did you ever see a goblin,
Stomp this way or that?

Stomp this way or that way,
Or this way or that way,
Did you ever see a goblin
Stomp this way or that?

ADDITIONAL VERSES...

Did you ever see a fairy...
Dance this way or that?

Did you ever see an old witch...
Fly this way or that?

Did you ever see a black cat...
Pounce this way or that

Did you ever see a night owl...
Sleep this way or that?

Did you ever see a spider...
Crawl this way or that?

Did you ever see a scarecrow...
Lean this way or that?

Did you ever see a pumpkin...
Roll this way or that?

Pumpkin Art

PUMPKIN TOTEM POLE

MATERIALS YOU WILL NEED
one small pumpkin for each child
knife
toothpicks
construction paper scraps
yarn
scissors

WHAT TO DO
1. Remove the stems from the pumpkins. Cut tops flat so the pumpkins will stack easily.
2. Design the pumpkin's face by cutting the construction paper scraps into colorful eyes, nose and mouth. Attach them to the pumpkin with toothpicks.
3. For hair, attach pre-cut strands of yarn to the pumpkin with toothpicks.
4. Stack the finished pumpkins one on top of another with the largest on the bottom, smallest on the top to make a pumpkin totem pole.
5. Have a story-time to create tales and adventures about each pumpkin in the totem pole.

Variation: Use marshmallows, Cheerios, raisin, and other food items to design a pumpkin face instead of construction paper.

TEAR A GHOST

MATERIALS YOU WILL NEED
newspaper or newsprint

WHAT TO DO
1. Practice tearing paper before you begin. Tear only a little at a time, slowly. Keep the tear between your fingers, rather than letting it get ahead of you.
2. Tear a ghost. Draw or tear his eyes and mouth.
3. Hang him from the ceiling so he can float through the air.

PLANT YOUR PUMPKIN SEEDS

MATERIALS YOU WILL NEED
pumpkin seeds
clean, small, empty milk container
potting soil
construction paper scraps
crayons (optional)
scissors
staples
water and sunshine

WHAT TO DO
1. Staple precut construction paper onto the sides of a small milk container. Decorate the sides with paper scraps or crayons.
2. Fill the container with potting soil.
3. Plant your pumpkin seed in the soil.
4. Water just enough to keep the soil moist. Place in a sunny spot to watch the seeds sprout and grow.

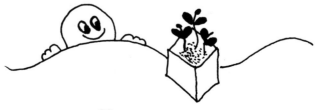

FINGER PAINT A PUMPKIN

MATERIALS YOU WILL NEED
   orange finger paint
   newsprint, butcher paper or construction paper
   newspaper to protect the table
   yellow construction paper or cellophane
   scissors

WHAT TO DO
1.   Prepare the area for finger painting.
2.   Finger paint a pumpkin. Pull your fingers through
     the paint to create the lines in a pumpkin. Set it aside
     to dry.
3.   Cut the pumpkin into a circle.
4.   Make a pumpkin face one of two ways:
     (a) Using yellow construction paper and scissors,
         cut out eyes, nose and mouth. Glue them ont
         the pumpkin.
     (b) Cut holes for the eyes, nose and mouth. On the
         back of the pumpkin, tape yellow cellophane to
         cover the holes. Hang the pumpkin in the
         window where it will "glow."

A CAT BEHIND A PUMPKIN

MATERIALS YOU WILL NEED
   one 9x12" sheet orange construction paper
   one 9x12" sheet black construction paper
   yellow and green construction paper scraps
   glue
   scissors

WHAT TO DO
1.   Cut a big, round, orange pumpkin.
2.   Cut a green stem and yellow eyes, nose and mouth.
     Glue them to the pumpkin.
3.   Cut out a head, tail, and two legs of a black cat. (see
     illustration)
4.   Glue the cat *behind* the pumpkin.
5.   From scraps, cut details for the cat's face. Glue them
     on.

MASK ON A STICK
MATERIAL YOU WILL NEED
    construction paper scraps
    scissors
    glue
    12" stick or dowel rod
    glitter
    an adult to supervise the marking of the holes for the
    eyes.
WHAT TO DO
1. Cut a 4 or 5 inch circle, oval or square.
2. Cut two eye holes. An adult should supervise.
3. Decorate the mask with construction paper designs.
    Fold, bend, fray, or curl small scraps, them glue them
    onto the mask.
4. Glue the stick to the back side of the mask so it can
    be held in front of the face.
5. Have a parade around the room to show off all of the
    fancy masks.

WEAVE A HALLOWEEN PLACEMENT
MATERIALS YOU WILL NEED
    one 9x12" sheet black construction paper
    one 9x12" sheet orange construction paper
    glue
    scissors

WHAT TO DO
1. Draw a 1 inch border around the edge of the black
    paper. Do not cut past this margin (see number 2).
2. Cut straight, parallel lines from top to bottom of the
    page about 1 inch apart. Stop at the 1" border.
3. Cut nine 1x12" orange strips.
4. Weave the strips over and under through the black
    mat.
5. Put a dab of glue on the end of each woven strip to
    hold it in place.
6. Use this mat at your Halloween party!

35

HALLOWEEN OWL

MATERIALS YOU WILL NEED

one 12x18" sheet of construction paper
one 9x12" sheet of brown construction paper
one 9x12" sheet of orange construction paper
construction paper scraps
scissors
glue

WHAT TO DO

1. Cut the brown 9x12" paper to a 9x9" square.
2. Fold in three corners approximately 3 inches, making the top knot and wings.
3. Fringe the edges of the three corners to make "feathers."
4. Front he scraps, cut eyes, feet and a triangle beak. Glue them onto the owl.
5. Cut out a fat orange pumpkin. From scraps, cut eyes, nose, and mouth, then glue them on the pumpkin.
6. Set the owl on top of the pumpkin and glue them both onto the 12x18" construction paper.

HALLOWEEN TREE

MATERIALS YOU WILL NEED
branch
coffee can, decorated
sand
string or paper clips

WHAT TO DO

1. Fill a coffee can with sand, then stand the branch in it.
2. Hang your bats, cats, witches, ghosts, and other art on strings from the Halloween tree. Unbend a paper clip if you need a hook.

PUMPKIN IN A WINDOW

MATERIALS YOU WILL NEED

    two 9x12" sheets orange construction paper
    two 12" lengths of waxed paper
    dull knife
    one red, yellow and orange crayon
    iron
    newspaper and paper towels
    scissors
    glue
    an adult to supervise use of the iron

WHAT TO DO

1. Hold the 2 orange sheets together to cut out 2 pumpkins, their eyes, nose and mouth at one time.
2. In a safe area, heat an iron to a low setting. Make sure an adult is in charge.
3. With the knife, shave bits of red, yellow, and orange from the side of a crayon onto one piece of the waxed paper.
4. Lay the other piece of waxed paper on top of the crayon shavings.
5. Check! Make sure the crayon shavings are aligned with the pumpkin's eyes, nose and mouth so they will "shine" through those openings once it is all put together.
6. Prepare the ironing station. First put down a layer of thick newspaper, then a paper towel. Place the waxed paper and crayon shavings on the paper towel, then cover it with another towel to protect the iron.
7. Set the iron on the paper towel for only a few seconds. Check to see if the crayon has melted. If need be, iron again for a few seconds, then allow the paper to cool.
8. Glue the waxed paper between the two pumpkins. Arrange it so the melted crayon shows through the eyes, nose and mouth of the pumpkin.
9. Trim the excess waxed paper to the edges of the pumpkin.
10. Hang the pumpkin in the window where it will catch the sunlight and "glow."

MOUSE PUZZLE IN A PUMPKIN

MATERIALS YOU WILL NEED
 two 9x12" sheets orange construction paper
 hole puncher
 yarn and tape
 crayons or magic markers
 two 9x12" sheets brown construction paper
 scissors
 glue

WHAT TO DO
1. Hold two orange sheet of construction paper together, and cut out 2 pumpkins at one time for a front and a back.
2. Draw a face on one of the pumpkins.
3. Holding the front and back of the pumpkin together, punch holes 1/2 inch from the 2-3 inches apart all around the pumpkin except the top.
4. Tape one end of the yarn for easy sewing. Sew the front and back of the pumpkin together. Allow enough yarn at the top to tie a handle. Remember...the top of the pumpkin remains open.
5. Now make the puzzle. Cut a large teardrop shape from one of the sheets of brown paper.
6. Cut a large circle from the other sheet of brown paper.
7. Glue the circle to the top of the teardrop to make the ear of the mouse. From the brown scraps, cut and glue on a tail.
8. Cut the mouse into four large pieces to make the puzzle. Adult assistance may be needed.
9. Store the puzzle in the pumpkin until you are ready to put it together to see who lives in the pumpkin.
10. Other puzzles will fit, too.

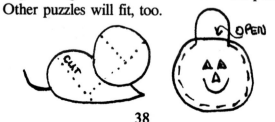

COTTON GHOSTS IN A HAUNTED HOUSE

MATERIALS YOU WILL NEED
one 9x12" sheet black construction paper
scissors
white chalk
cotton
glue

WHAT TO DO
1. Cut the shape of a haunted house from black construction paper. See figure 1.
2. Cut a door in a haunted house which will open and close. See figure 2.
3. Using white chalk, draw windows on the haunted house. See figure 3.
4. Gently pull a cotton ball into the shape of a ghost. Make as many ghosts as you wish.
5. Cut tiny black eyes from constrution paper scraps. Glue them onto the ghosts.
6. Glue the ghosts onto the haunted house. Hide one of the ghosts behind the haunted door.

VARIATION: Let all of the children paricipate in making one very large haunted house. Glue their ghosts on, in and around it.

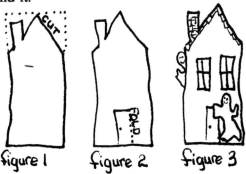

figure 1   figure 2   figure 3

CHARCOAL A GOBLIN

MATERIALS YOU WILL NEED
   charcoal sticks
   12x18" sheet of construction paper

WHAT TO DO
1.   Read "Five Little Goblins" on page 18, then "The Goblin" on page 13.
2.   Encourage each child to *create* a goblin on his paper using charcoal.
3.   Have each child write a story about his goblin.

BEAN BAG GHOST

MATERIALS YOU WILL NEED
   6x6" piece of cloth
   string
   kidney beans
   felt tip pen
   12x18" paper

WHAT TO DO
1.   Place a few beans in the center of the material.
2.   Gather the edges and tie the beans in the center with a string. If you wish, use a felt tip pen to draw a face on the ghost.
3.   Draw a haunted house with a felt tip pen on the 12x18" paper.
4.   Set a few ground rules and toss the ghost bean bags at the haunted house.

BLACK CAT NOISE MAKERS

MATERIALS YOU WILL NEED

two paper plates
one tongue depressor
one 2" square of black construction paper
yellow construction paper scraps
black tempera paint and brush
stapler
glue
kidney beans

WHAT TO DO

1. Paint the paper plates black and let them dry.
2. Cut the 2" black squares corner to corner, or diagonally, to make two triangle ears. Staple the ears to the plates.
3. Put a few kidney beans between the two plates and the tongue depressor under the cat's chin for a handle. Finish stapling the two plates together.
4. Glue on yellow construction paper details for a face.
5. Give it a shake!
6. This is also a great way to make stick puppets. Create different characters, staple them to the tongue depressor and have your own Halloween puppet show!

PLAY DOUGH PUMPKIN PATCH

MATERIALS YOU WILL NEED

    3 cups flour
    1 cup salt
    1 cup water
    2 tbs. salad oil
    red, yellow and green food coloring
    bowl
    spoons
    measuring cup and spoons
    waxed paper

WHAT TO DO

1. Mix the flour, salt, water and salad oil in the bowl.
2. Divide the dough into three portions, the third being smaller than the first two. Add equal drops of red and yellow to one of the portions to make orange dough. Add green food coloring drops to the smaller portion of the dough. Add no color to the third portion.
3. Divide the children into three groups. Group I makes the orange, round pumpkins. Group II makes the green leaves and vines. Group III makes the ghosts and spiders and other Halloween characters hiding in the pumpkin patch. Arrange the figures on waxed paper.
4. Display the pumpkin patch. Take turns inventing stories about "Way Down Yonder in the Pumpkin Patch..."

SEW A GHOST

MATERIALS YOU WILL NEED
 an old sheet or pillow case
 scissors
 pencil
 needle and thread
 an adult to supervise sewing and cutting eye holes

WHAT TO DO
1. Lay two pieces of material together on the floor. Have the "ghost" lie down on the material with arms out. Trace around the body, leaving lots of room for a flowing, roomy ghost costume.
2. Cut the material on the traced line.
3. Demonstrate a simple running stitch and safe sewing. Sew large running stitches all the way around the border, except along the bottom.
4. Try on the costume. Draw and cut the eye holes. Be careful!
5. Have the "ghosts" write a play and perform in costume!

VARIATION: For a crinkly, wrinkly, noisy ghost, use butcher paper. Follow the same procedure as above. Staple the edges together.

PUMPKIN FINGER PUPPETS

MATERIALS YOU WILL NEED
   orange construction paper or felt
   yellow and green construction paper scraps
   scissors
   glue

WHAT TO DO
1. Cut an orange, round pumpkin 1" to 2" high.
2. Cut then glue on a green stem and yellow eyes, nose and mouth.
3. On the back, glue a 1/4" strip on the ends, leaving enough room for a finger to fit under it.

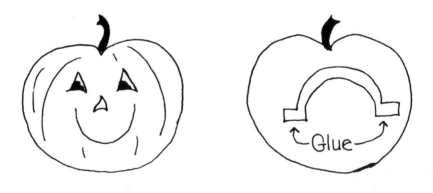

FRONT   BACK

STUFF A WITCH

MATERIALS YOU WILL NEED

three 12x18" sheets black construction paper
on 5x5" square pink construction paper
crayons
scissors
stapler
glue
four pre-cut 18" strands of yarn
newspaper

WHAT TO DO

1. Cut a pink circle for the witch's face. Draw eyes, nose and mouth with crayon.
2. Glue pre-cut strands of yarn to witch's head for hair.
3. Cut a tall triangular hat for the witch. Glue it to the witch's head. Set it aside to dry.
4. Fold *two* black pieces of construction paper in half lengthwise.
5. Cut out the witch's dress as shown in figure 1. Do not cut on the fold.
6. Open the two dress parts and staple them together around the edges, leaving an opening at the top or neck.
7. Stuff small bits of wrinkled newspaper into the opening of the dress.
8. Attach the witch's head to the dres at the neck with a staple or glue.
9. From remaining scraps, cut and glue on optional details such as feet, hands, etc.
10. Read the poem, "The Old Witch," on page 19 as your witch rides across the sky.

OPEN, STAPLE, STUFF

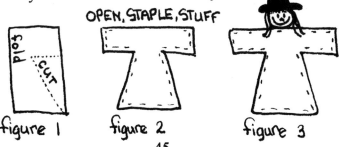

figure 1   figure 2   figure 3

Pumpkin Games

1, 2, 3, 4
5, 6, ...

WITCH, WHERE'S YOUR BROOM?

MATERIALS YOU WILL NEED
   one chair
   a small object representing a broom

HOW TO PLAY
1. Choose one child to be a witch to sit in a chair in the center. The rest of the children sit around in a circle.
2. Place a "broom" under the witch's chair.
3. The witch covers her eyes.
4. One person sneaks quietly to the chair and takes the witch's broom, returns to the circle, and hides the broom behind his back. All other players hide their hands behind their backs also to look as if they too have the broom.
5. When everyone is ready, all together say, "Witch, witch, where's your broom?"
6. The witch has three chances to find the broom by guessing which child has it hidden behind his back.
7. If the witch *cannot* guess where the broom is hiding, the child with the broom goes to the chair to become the new witch. If the witch *does* guess who has the broom, she remains the witch for another turn.

SPIN THE HALLOWEEN BOTTLE

MATERIALS YOU WILL NEED
    plastic bottle
    paper
    pencil

HOW TO PLAY
1. Write names (or draw pictures for younger children) of Halloween characters on separate pieces of paper. You can include ghosts, goblins, witches, brooms, doorbells, trick-or-treaters, bats, cats, moon, elves, or scarecrows to name only a few. Fold and place the papers in the bottle.
2. All players sit in a circle.
3. Spin the bottle.
4. When the bottle stops spinning, it will point to a child. He must select one paper from the bottle, then act out his Halloween character for the rest of the children to guess.
5. Whoever guesses correctly, spins the bottle for the next game.
6. If the bottle points to a child who has alread had a turn, spin again.

HALLOWEEN MATCH

MATERIALS YOU WILL NEED
   18 sheets of 9x12" construction paper
   felt tip pen

HOW TO PLAY
1.   Write each of the letters from the word HALLOWEEN on separate sheets of paper *twice*.
2.   Pass one set of HALLOWEEN letters to 9 children, one letter to each child.
3.   Ask those 9 children to leave the room while you hide the matching set of letters in different spots.
4.   Then have the 9 children return to search for their letter's match. Explain if another letter is found, it must be left in its place without telling its location. If a child turns in a mismatch, he must rehide the card and continue the search.
5.   When all the cards are found and matched, start the game over, giving each child a new letter to find. If there are more than 9 players, give other children a turn.

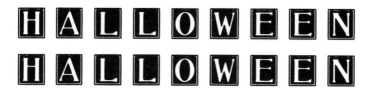

PUT THE FELT NOSE ON THE PUMPKIN

MATERIALS YOU WILL NEED
one large, orange, felt pumpkin face
one felt nose for each player
blindfold

HOW TO PLAY
1. Hang the pumpkin within reach of the children.
2. Pass out one pumpkin nose to each player.
3. Cover the first player's eyes with the blindfold.
4. Gently spin the child around.
5. Let the child try to put his nose on the pumpkin's nose.
6. Give each child a turn and see who can place it the closest.

HALLOWEEN SEQUENCE POSTERS
MATERIALS YOU WILL NEED
Make up a set of posters depicting a sequence of Halloween events, such as:
planting pumpkin seeds,
the steps to carving jack-o'-lanterns,
putting on a costume,
or trick or treating safely.

HOW TO PLAY
1. Discuss each poster picture with the children.
2. Ask one child to arrange them in the proper order.
3. Another child can describe a scene to the others.
4. If need be, lend assistance in arranging the posters in proper order and in describing them.

HIDE THE GHOST

MATERIALS YOU WILL NEED
one little ghost cut from a 9x12" sheet of construction paper

HOW TO PLAY
1. Five children leave the room.
2. Hide the ghost in the room.
3. The five children return to the room to search for the ghost. If they are close to the hiding place of the ghost, clap loudly. If they are far from the ghost, clap softly.
4. The player to find the ghost is the winner and hides the ghost for the next game. Choose five new players to be "seekers" for the next game.

PASS THE PUMPKINS

MATERIALS YOU WILL NEED
two bean bag pumpkins

HOW TO PLAY
1. Form two circles.
2. One leader in each circle holds a pumpkin. On "Go," each begins passing the pumpkin around the circle.
3. The first circle to have the pumpkin back to the leader is the winner.

TELL A PUMPKIN TALE

MATERIALS YOU WILL NEED
"The Pumpkin Story Starter" provided below.

WHAT TO DO
1. Read the story starter to the children. When finished, ask the children to either draw or tell an ending ot the story.
2. Be sure to record thier creative effort so it can be read again and again, or sent home to be shared with the family. Also, you can jot down each child's story ending on his or her art work.

The Pumpkin STORY STARTER

Once upon a time there was a pumpkin patch tucked in the hills of a far away land called Pumple. There, pumpkins grew so thick and so fat and so orange that they were the finest pumpkins in the world. People would come great distances for a pumpkin from the Pumple pumpkin patch. And whoever picked a Pumple pumpkin was immediately granted three magic wishes. They would ask for anything their hearts desired.

One day, a little boy named Nathan and his sister Rebecca arrived in the land of Pumple. It was their dream to have a Pumple pumpkin. When they finally came to the pumpkin patch, they couldn't believe what they saw...

(Here, the children finish the story any way they wish.)

WITCHES, GHOSTS AND GOBLINS

MATERIALS YOU WILL NEED
    large playing field or gym

HOW TO PLAY
1. Designate two parallel lines 25 feet apart as boundaries or "safe" lines.
2. Have all the children line up on one of the safe lines. Select three children to be IT. One will be a witch, one will be a ghost, and one will be a goblin. The three that are selected to be It, move to the center between the safe lines.
3. Have the rest of children on the line "count off" witch, ghost or goblin until all are assigned.
4. Now the game begins. One of the three children that are IT calls out, "The witches are out tonight," "The ghosts are out tonight," or "The goblins are out tonight." The group that is named runs to the opposite line trying to avoid being tagged.
5. If a player is tagged, he joins the children in the center to help them tag other players.
6. If "Halloween Scramble" is called, *everyone* left on the line runs to the opposite side.
7. The last three players caught are the winners and IT in the next game.

Pumpkin Treats

AUNT LINDA'S
SUGAR COOKIE GHOSTS

MATERIALS YOU WILL NEED

2 cups white flour	1 cup butter or margarine
1 cup whole wheat flour	1 egg
1 cup sugar	3 tbsp. light cream or
1-1/2 tsp. baking powder	evap. milk
1/2 tsp. salt	1 tsp. vanilla

measuring cups and spoons
mixing bowl
mixer and spoon
pastry cloth and rolling pin
dull knife or cookie cutters
cookie sheet
oven
cooling racks

WHAT TO DO

1. In large bowl, combine flour, sugar, baking powder and salt. With mixer, cut in the butter until crumbly. Stir in egg, cream and vanilla. Blend well. If desired, refrigerate the dough.
2. Roll our the dough onto a floured cloth to 1/8" thickness. With a dull knife, cut dough into small ghost shapes, or use Halloween cookie cutters to shape the dough.
3. Place on ungreased cookie sheet. Sprinkle sugar on top.
4. Bake at 400° for 5-8 minutes, then cool the cookies on a cooling rack. You can decorate these cookies with frosting if you wish.
5. DELICIOUS!

FRIED PUMPKIN SEEDS

MATERIALS YOU WILL NEED
   pumpkin seeds from your carved pumpkin
   2 tbsp. butter or margarine
   salt
   spoon
   electric skillet
   cookie sheet
   oven

WHAT TO DO
1.   Melt the butter in electric skillet at 325°.
2.   Stir in the pumpkin seeds.
3.   Sprinkle salt over the top of the seeds.
4.   Fry the seeds for 15 minutes, stirring constantly. Salt again twice.
5.   Spoon seeds onto cookie sheet. Bake in oven at 350° for 5-10 minutes.
6.   Serve the seeds warm on the Halloween Placemat you wove following directions on page 35.

CREAM CHEESE GHOSTS
WITH CRACKERS

INGREDIENTS YOU WILL NEED

one 8-oz. package cream cheese, softened
raisins
crackers
waxed paper

WHAT TO DO

1. Wash hands.
2. Divide cream cheese into small balls. Give one to each child.
3. Mold cheese into tiny ghosts with fingers.
4. Place each ghost on a cracker.
5. Add two raisin eyes.
6. Serve the crackers at the Halloween party!

PEANUT GHOSTS

INGREDIENTS YOU WILL NEED
one bag of peanuts in the shell
fine tipped marking pens
small paper cups

WHAT TO DO
1. Give each child a handful of peanuts, a marking pen and a cup.
2. Draw a tiny ghost face on each peanut shell.
3. Place the peanuts in the cup.
4. Have each child tell a "ghost story" before you gobble them up!

HALLOWEEN PUNCH

INGREDIENTS YOU WILL NEED
1 large can orange juice (46 oz.)
1 large can pineapple juice
1 quart orange sherbet
2 quarts ginger ale
punch bowl or container
cups

WHAT TO DO
1. Mix orange juice, pineapple juice, and sherbet.
2. Chill.
3. Just before serving, add ginger ale.
4. Pour into cups and serve.

PUMPKIN SOUP

INGREDIENTS YOU WILL NEED

      6 cups or 4 lbs. cooked, fresh pumpkin
      6 cups scalded milk
      2 tbsp. butter
      2 tbsp. brown sugar or white sugar
      salt and pepper
      nutmeg and cinnamon
      tiny pinch saffron
      1 cup finely chopped julienned ham
      1 large soup pot
      stirring spoon
      hot pad

WHAT TO DO

1.   Mix ingredients in soup pot and heat. DO NOT BOIL.
2.   Serve immediately. Makes about 8 cups.

59

PUMPKIN BREAD

INGREDIENTS YOU WILL NEED
  3-1/2 cups unsifted all purpose flour
  2 tsp. cinnamon
  1 tsp. salt
  1/2 tsp. double-acting baking powder
  1/2 tsp. ground allspice
  2 1/3 cups sugar
  1 cup salad oil
  4 eggs
  1/3 cup water
  one 16-oz. can pumpkin
  1/2 cup nutmeat or raisins
  two 9x5" loaf pans
  2 bowls
  spoon and spatula
  hot pad
  knife

WHAT TO DO
1. Preheat oven to 350°F. Grease pans and set aside.
2. Combine flour, cinnamon, salt, baking powder and allspice in bowl. Set aside.
3. In another bowl, beat sugar and oil. Add eggs, water and pumpkin. Stir together.
4. Gradually add dry ingredients and stir just until blended.
5. Stir in nuts or raisins, if desired.
6. Pour batter into loaf pans and bake for 55-60 minutes, or until knife inserted in center comes out clean.
7. Cool on wire racks for 10 minutes before removing from pan. Then, cool completely.
8. Serve this delicious pumpkin treat with cream cheese or butter.

CARAMEL APPLES

INGREDIENTS YOU WILL NEED
    4-6 medium sized apples
    1 pound caramels
    2 tbsp. water
    4-6 popsicle sticks or skewers
    double boiler
    hot pads
    knife
    greased waxed paper or tinfoil

WHAT TO DO
1. Wash apples.
2. Push popsicle sticks into apples at stems.
3. Heat caramel and water in double boiler until melted.
4. Dip apple into caramel sauce. Hold stick and twirl apple until covered and coated with caramel.
5. Place apples on waxed paper to set. If refrigerated, they will set in a few minutes.

PUMPKIN PANCAKES

INGREDIENTS YOU WILL NEED
2 cups buttermilk baking mix
2 eggs
1 cup milk
1/2 cup pumpkin
1/4 cup water

WHAT TO DO
1. Mix the first three ingredients together.
2. Gently stir in pumpkin.
3. Add water. Blend.
4. Cook on a hot griddle until pancakes are dry around edges. Flip, then cook until brown.
5. Batter can be easily poured into Halloween shapes using a spoon. Pour slowly!
6. Serve with any pancake topping or just plain.

SUSAN'S TOOTSIE ROLL GHOSTS

INGREDIENTS YOU WILL NEED
    one Tootsie Roll sucker per child
    one white kleenex tissue per child
    string
    scissors
    black felt tip marking pen

WHAT TO DO
1. Cover the tootsie roll with a kleenex.
2. With a string, tie the tissue onto the stick just under the sucker.
3. Draw the ghost's eyes, nose and mouth with black marking pen.
4. Let the children enjoy the ghostly treat while you read the poem "Who's Afraid" on page 10.

WHAT IS REAL? WHAT IS PRETEND?

Halloween is the perfect time of the year to explain to young children the difference between **real** and **pretend**. Eliminate some of the awe and wonder, and maybe even fear, of ghosts and goblins associated with Halloween night. Here's an activity which might help:

> After discussing the names things that are **real** and **pretend**, make two lists (a picture list for children who cannot read): one of things that are real, and one of things that are not real (or pretend). Display it or keep it handy so you can refer to it throughout the holiday.

YOUR OWN PUMPKIN NOTES

CREDITS

"What Is It?" by Aileen Fisher
reprinted by permission of Abalard-Schuman, New York, from RUNNY DAYS, SUNNY DAYS, copyright 1958

"Riddles: What Am I?" by Dorothy Aldis
reprinted by permission of G.P. Putnam's Sons from HOP, SKIP AND JUMP!, copyright 1934, copyright renewed 1961 by Dorothy Aldis.

"Halloween Song" by Marjorie Barrows
reprinted by permission of "Child Life Magazine", copyright 1927, 1958 by Rand McNally & Company

Mrs. Helen Fish, Mr. Margaret Schwimmer, and Mrs. Paula Stout contributed ideas printed in THE PUMPKIN BOOK.

TO ALL OF THE ABOVE, and to Dan Higgins, Ron Schultz, Lib Hyatt, John Pola, Bob and Ann Hammond, Janet Douglas, Florence Higgins, Bill Olson, Betty Baldwin, and Janet Albright, thank you for helping the pumpkin grow.

The PUMPKIN BOOK

Written and published by Susan Olson Higgins
P.O. Box 139
Shasta, CA 96087
PUMPKIN PRESS

P.O. Box 139
Shasta, CA 96087